ANCIENT WORLDS

ANCIENT LAWS: THE WEIRD AND THE DEADLY

Martin Gitlin

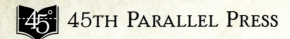

45th Parallel Press

Published in the United States of America by Cherry Lake Publishing Group
Ann Arbor, Michigan
www.cherrylakepublishing.com

Reading Adviser: Beth Walker Gambro, MS, Ed., Reading Consultant, Yorkville, IL

Photo Credits: © r.classen/Shutterstock, cover, title page; © Renata Sedmakova/Shutterstock. 5; © Darrin Klimek/iStock.com, 7; © Historic Collection/Alamy Stock Photo, 8; © Lanmas/Alamy Stock Photo, 11; © Francesca Pianzola/Shutterstock, 12; © Dima Moroz/Shutterstock, 14; © Claudine Van Massenhove/Shutterstock, 16; © Eakachai Leesin/Shutterstock, 18; Yan Li-pen, Public domain, via Wikimedia Commons, 20; © Joe Wabe/Shutterstock, 22; © Dimitrios P/Shutterstock, 24; © Songquan Deng/Shutterstock, 27; © ded pixto/Shutterstock, 28; Theodoor van Thulden, Public domain, via Wikimedia Commons, 30

Graphic Element Credits: Graphic Element Credits: Cover, multiple interior pages: © Andrey_Kuzmin/Shutterstock, © cajoer/Shutterstock, © GUSAK OLENA/Shutterstock, © Eky Studio/Shutterstock

Copyright © 2025 by Cherry Lake Publishing Group
All rights reserved. No part of this book may be reproduced or utilized
in any form or by any means without written permission from the publisher.
45TH Parallel Press is an imprint of Cherry Lake Publishing Group.

Library of Congress Cataloging-in-Publication Data has been filed and is available at catalog.loc.gov.

Cherry Lake Publishing Group would like to acknowledge the work of the Partnership for 21st Century Learning, a Network of Battelle for Kids. Please visit http://www.battelleforkids.org/networks/p21 for more information.

Printed in the United States of America

Note from publisher: Websites change regularly, and their future contents are outside of our control.
Supervise children when conducting any recommended online searches for extended learning opportunities.

About the Author
Martin Gitlin is an educational book author based in Connecticut. He won more than 45 awards as a newspaper journalist from 1991 to 2002. Included was a first-place award from the Associated Press. That organization voted him as one of the top four feature writers in Ohio in 2002. Martin has had about 250 books published since 2006. Most of them were written for students. He has authored many books about history.

TABLE OF CONTENTS

Introduction 4

Chapter 1: The Terrible Twelve Tables 8

Chapter 2: The Death Penalty 12

Chapter 3: Being Short 16

Chapter 4: Forced to Drink Ink 20

Chapter 5: The Greek Island of Delos 24

Chapter 6: Purple Reign 28

Glossary 32
Learn More 32
Index 32

INTRODUCTION

In ancient times, **crucifixion** was a form of public punishment. It was when a person was killed on a cross. It happened to Jesus of Nazareth. Christians follow his teachings.

Laws are meant to be fair. They're meant to ensure order. People break laws. They need to be punished. Punishments should be fair. They should fit the crime. But what is fair punishment? It's hard to decide that. It depends on lawmakers. Each person judges crimes differently. Laws vary greatly from country to country.

The ancient world had many strange laws. Ancient thinking is tough to understand. It's hard to believe certain actions were once **illegal**. Illegal means against the law.

Ancient punishments were cruel. Lawbreakers were often killed. Or they had limbs cut off. Some were tortured. Such laws were seen as **deterrents**. Deterrents are meant to stop behaviors. Ancient people thought tough punishments would stop crimes.

Times have changed. So have laws. And so have punishments. They've evolved. They've become less strict. Many crimes in ancient times are legal today. Modern punishments are often less harsh. Today, some nations have no death **penalty**. Penalty is punishment. Many **sentences** cause no physical pain. People may just get sent to jail. Sentences are punishments. They're decided by judges.

People need to follow laws. Crimes need to be punished. That was the idea in ancient times. It's the same today. But what is a crime? Ancient lawmakers had some weird ideas. Some ideas were deadly.

Today, there are different sentences for different crimes. Often, harsher crimes have longer sentences.

CHAPTER ONE

The Twelve Tables gave men power. Men had power over their wives. They had power over their children.

The Terrible Twelve Tables

Ancient Rome was advanced for its time. Romans created many great things. They made great impacts. They gave much to modern society. One example was **sanitation**. Sanitation is about keeping places clean. It includes clean water. It includes removing waste. It keeps people healthy. It stops people from getting sick.

They created a 365-day calendar. This calendar is still used today. They also introduced foods. Examples are pears and peas.

Ancient Rome was a nation of laws. A famous code was **decreed**. Decree means an official order. This happened in 450–451 BCE. The code was called the Twelve Tables.

The Twelve Tables had laws. Some still make sense. One said the accused must appear in court. This ensured a fair trial. Another outlawed night meetings.

But other laws were strange. And their punishments were cruel. One example was the crime of **fraud**. Fraud is lying. The punishment was death.

What was the most bizarre law? That was writing or singing insults. People couldn't insult others. The Twelve Tables made this illegal. Anyone who did this was put to death.

In ancient times, most executions were public. People gathered to watch them.

CHAPTER TWO

Owning land in ancient times gave people more power. They could farm. They could make money off the land.

The Death Penalty

Draco lived in the 7th century BCE. He inspired a modern word. The word *draconian* came from his name. It means "too harsh." This made sense. Draco was harsh. He wrote a brutal set of laws. Lawbreakers were punished with death.

Draco was not a ruler. But he had a lot of power. He was highly educated. He had an important goal. He wanted to create order. He did this for Athens. Athens was an ancient Greek city.

There were many fights. Nobody knew how to deal with them. There were no judges. There were no courts. There were no punishments. Victims or their families decided punishments. They decided their own justice. This caused problems. People did what they wanted. Things got messy.

So Draco went to work. He created a series of laws. But his laws were unfair. They favored rich landowners.

That was not the worst part. His laws were cruel. Many small crimes were punished by death. People stole animals. They stole apples. They forgot to pay taxes. Draconian law put them to death. This didn't make sense. It created fear.

Draco's laws didn't last long. Solon was a Greek leader. He ended Draco's laws. He stopped nearly every death penalty. He kept it for murder. But Draco had made his mark. His name is still used today.

Solon was a Greek leader and poet.

A NICE STORY

The tale of Damon and Pythias is fiction. It is set in ancient times. It's about friendship. Damon and Pythias were best friends.

One day, Pythias angered Dionysius. Dionysius was a Greek **tyrant**. Tyrants are harsh rulers. Dionysius jailed Pythias. He sentenced him to death. Damon tried to get him released. He failed. The 2 friends spoke. Pythias wanted to see his mother. But his mother lived far away.

Damon visited Dionysius. He asked to replace Pythias in prison. If Pythias didn't return, Damon would take his place. He offered to be put to death. He trusted Pythias would come back.

Pythias at first refused. But Damon insisted. So Pythias left. He went to say goodbye to his mother.

Dionysius told Damon that Pythius would not return. But Damon trusted Pythias. Pythius almost didn't return on time. He was kidnapped. He was tied to a tree. He escaped. He almost drowned. He finally returned. Damon was just about to be killed. Dionysius was shocked. He was impressed. He let both men free.

CHAPTER THREE

Emperor Qin Shi Huang was only the **emperor** of China for 11 years. An emperor is a ruler. He started the Qin Dynasty.

Being Short

Dynasties are ruling families. They ruled ancient China. The Qin Dynasty of China lasted just 15 years. It was from 221 to 206 BCE. But its laws are still talked about today. They were that strange.

They were the 18 Laws of Qin. They were written on bamboo strips. They were dug up in 1975. What was found is hard to believe.

Qin laws had a different way of judging adulthood. It's not based on age. It was centered on height. It favored short people. Men 5 feet (1.5 meters) or shorter were found innocent. They couldn't be **convicted** of crimes. Convicted means to be found guilty. Qin Shi Huang was the leader of the Qin Dynasty. He was exactly that height. The same was true for women. Those 4 feet, 10 inches (1.5 m) and shorter were safe.

Qin men had to control their emotions. They couldn't cry. They were punished for doing so. The punishment was odd. Crying men had their beards shaved. Their eyebrows were also shaved. The Qin Dynasty was known for its warriors. Men were meant to be strong. Those who cried were cowards. Such emotion was seen as weakness.

Some Qin penalties seem too light today. What if a man bit off another person's nose or ear? His beard was cut off. It's the same punishment for crying. This doesn't seem fair.

Different cultures view emotions in different ways. This was true in ancient times. It is true now.

MYSTERY SOLVED OR UNSOLVED?

There was a mummy. It was known as Gebelein Man. He was well-preserved. Preserved means saved. His remains were displayed. They were in the British Museum. They were in the early Egypt gallery. They were there for 100 years.

Experts studied him. Gebelein Man was buried around 3500 BCE. His name is from the Gebelein burial site. The site is in upper Egypt. The dry sand helped preserve his bones. That made it easier to learn about him. Experts wondered what killed him.

Gebelein Man was taken to the Bupa Cromwell Hospital. This hospital is in London. This happened in 2012, Experts took x-rays. It's believed to be the first x-ray of an ancient mummy.

Much was learned. Gebelein Man was 18 to 21 years old when he died. He didn't die from sickness. There was damage to his shoulder blade and rib. This proves he was stabbed. It looked like a single stab wound. It reached deep inside his body. His killer was likely put to death. Ancient laws against murder were harsher back then.

CHAPTER FOUR

Kaihuang is the name of an era in Chinese history. The Kaihuang Code had 12 chapters. It had 500 laws.

Forced to Drink Ink

What do modern folks get for bad handwriting? They might get laughed at. Or they might have to do a rewrite.

Not in ancient China. And not during the Sui Dynasty. The Sui Dynasty began 700 years after the Qin Dynasty. China had become more open. Anyone could be a government official. Before, only rich people had positions.

But China still had strange laws. They punished people for bad handwriting. This law targeted those who wanted to be government officials. People had to take a test. Taking tests is normal. But in ancient China, people had to write neatly. Those who didn't were punished. They were forced to drink ink! They had to swallow 7 ounces (207 milliliters).

People were told that test answers were sent to the emperor. This wasn't true. The emperor didn't grade tests. But bad handwriting insulted him. It showed disrespect. It offended the emperor.

This law was part of the Kaihuang Code. It's a series of laws. Wendi ordered the law. He was the first Sui Dynasty ruler. Drinking ink was a light punishment. There were harsher ones. Those who broke Sui law could be killed. And so could their children. Or they were beaten with bamboo.

Beautiful Chinese handwriting is still valued today. There are people who practice Chinese calligraphy.

ANCIENT RULES

Ancient Roman leaders wanted people to multiply. This had nothing to do with math. They tried to encourage people to have children. The goal was to strengthen society.

Roman leaders decreed a strange law. It was called *Lex Papia Poppaea*. It benefited married people.

Augustus was a Roman emperor. He supported the law. Couples with children got extra money.

There were some problems. The law punished rich unmarried people. It also punished some women. Some Roman women took **sacred** vows. Sacred means holy. These women vowed to not marry. They vowed to not have children. So they broke the law.

Many resisted. They thought the law was unfair. They complained. The law failed to boost birth rates. Even so, the law remained. It was finally taken away in the 5th century CE.

CHAPTER FIVE

The Delphic Oracle talked to Apollo. Apollo was the god of sun and light. He oversaw music, truth, and healing.

The Greek Island of Delos

Birth gives life. Death comes for everyone. But not in the 5th century BCE on Delos. Delos is a Greek island. Both death and birth were illegal there!

Ancient Greeks thought Delos was sacred. They wanted the island to be pure. It was ideal. It was a place to worship the gods. Greek leaders consulted a woman. The woman was called the Delphic Oracle. Oracles have special gifts. They talk to gods. They receive **prophecies**. Prophecies are predictions of the future. The Oracle decided all dead bodies must go. She said death was illegal. She said giving birth was illegal.

So the Greeks cleared the area. They targeted temple grave sites. They dug up dead bodies. They removed all the graves.

There were similar laws in modern times. Three French towns asked for cemeteries to be built. Their plans got rejected. Town leaders made death illegal. They did this in 2000. They did this to make a point. There was a mayor in Brazil. He made death illegal. He did this in 2005. He protested a lack of burial space.

People can still visit the ancient ruins of Delos today.

CHAPTER SIX

Julius Caesar and Caesar Augustus were Roman leaders. They decreed that only emperors could wear purple.

Purple Reign

Ancient Romans put on clean clothes. They did this in the morning. That isn't shocking. It's what people have done forever. But ancient Romans had to be careful when Nero was emperor. They couldn't wear purple. Those who did never returned home.

There was a law. Only emperors could wear purple. Anyone who broke this law was killed. Wearing purple had the same punishment as murder!

Purple was the most majestic color. Emperors wore purple **togas**. Togas are robes. Lower classes couldn't display such wealth. They had to know their place.

Purple dye was rare. It was costly. It had to be brought in from another kingdom. That kingdom was Phoenicia. About 10,000 shellfish were crushed to make the dye for the hem of 1 toga. The color was called Tyrian purple. It took 250,000 shellfish to produce 1 fluid ounce (30 mL) of dye.

There was a myth. Hercules was a Roman strongman. Some think he discovered the dye. It was said his dog once ate sea snails. The dog returned to Hercules. It had purple stains in his mouth.

This Hercules is different from the Greek demi-god Hercules. But both were strong!

VERY IMPORTANT PEOPLE

Solon was a lawmaker. He was also a poet. He was from Athens. His reforms lasted briefly. But he launched a great society. He impacted the Greek **economy**. An economy is a system of how money is made and used. He impacted Greek culture.

Solon was elected an archon. Archons are governors. This happened in 594 BCE. Athens was a mess. Farmers struggled. They owed money to rich landowners. Those who couldn't pay were sold. They became enslaved people. So did their wives and children.

Solon changed the law. He set all enslaved people in Athens free. He thought all people should be free in a democracy. Then everyone could participate in it. Solon also erased debts. That made him popular. He knew farmers didn't make enough money. He made Athens a powerful trade center. Athens' ships sailed to other lands. Solon urged foreign traders to live in Athens. That gave the economy a big boost.

Solon planted the seeds for democracy. He helped Athens grow. His council discussed public issues. All in the council could vote.

GLOSSARY

convicted (kuhn-VIKT-ed) having been found guilty of a crime by a judge or court of law

crucifixion (kroo-suh-FIK-shuhn) killed by nailing or tying wrists or hands and feet to a cross

decreed (dih-KREED) ordered what must be done

deterrents (dih-TUR-uhnts) things that discourage an action

dynasties (DYE-nuh-steez) ruling families

economy (ih-KAH-nuh-mee) the system of how money is made and used in a particular place

emperor (EM-puhr-uhr) the ruler of an empire

fraud (FRAWD) illegal use of lies or tricks against others for personal gain

illegal (ih-LEE-guhl) against the law

penalty (PEH-nuhl-tee) a punishment imposed for breaking a law or rule

prophecies (PRAH-fuh-seez) predictions or warnings of future events

sacred (SAY-krud) holy

sanitation (saa-nuh-TAY-shun) the practice of keeping people healthy through clean living conditions

sentences (SEN-tuhn-sez) punishments issued to people found guilty of crimes

togas (TOH-guhz) long, loose garments worn in ancient Rome

tyrant (TYE-ruhnt) a ruler who abuses their power by treating their subjects harshly

LEARN MORE

Dissected Lives. *The Wise King Hammurabi of Babylon and his Code of Law*. Newark, DE: Speedy Publishing, 2020.

Hubbard, Ben. *How We Lived in Ancient Times: Meet Everyday Children throughout History*. London, England: Welbeck Publishing, 2020

Search online with an adult:
Mr. Donn. Ancient Egypt for Kids: Law and Order Kiddle. Roman Law Facts for Kids

INDEX

Athens, 13–14, 31
Augustus, 23, 28

birth and death, 23, 25–26

Caesar, Julius, 28
China, 16–18, 20–22
crimes, 5–6, 7, 10, 14, 17–18, 21–22, 29
crucifixion, 4

Damon, 15
death penalty, 6, 10–11, 13–14, 29
Delos (island), 24–26, 27

Delphic Oracle, 24, 25
democracy, 31
Dionysius, 15
Draco, 13–14

emotions, 18

Gebelein Man, 19
Greece, 13–14, 15, 24–26, 27, 31

height, 17–18
Hercules, 30

jail sentences, 6, 7, 15

Kaihuang Code, 20–22

land ownership, 12, 14, 31
lawmakers, 5–6, 9–10, 13–14, 17, 21, 23, 25, 29, 31
Lex Papia Poppaea, 23

mummies, 19

punishments, 4–6, 10–11, 13–14, 18, 21–23, 29
purple, 28–30
Pythias, 15

Qin Dynasty, 16–18, 21
Qin Shi Huang, 16, 17

Rome, 8–10, 23, 28–30

social standing, 12, 14, 29, 31
Solon, 14, 31
Sui Dynasty, 21–22

Twelve Tables code, 8–11

writing, 10, 21–22

32